Arrive Alive Without Incident

A Motorcycle Driving Methodology & Risk-Ratio-Reduction Strategy

By

Robert Jaron

First published 2015

Printed by CreateSpace, Charleston South Carolina, U.S.A.

CreateSpace is a DBA of On-Demand Publishing LLC, part of the Amazon group of companies.

ISBN 9781482605181

www.arrivealivewithoutincident.com

To my wife, Debra:

Thank you for always demonstrating your love, support, and friendship through our journey together.

My eternal love

To my Brother, Gary:

Thank you for your answer to my primal and humble call for "help!" Specifically: thank you for your advice, pre-press editing assistance, and encouragement.

Dedication

Scott Logan Hudson

Beloved Brother

A Lady's 'soul mate'

Loyal Friend

Avid Music Lover

Adventurer

Natural Tour Guide

Worthy Scrabble Adversary

Prudent Sailor

Sept. 20 1956- July 6, 2009

RIP

Died in head-on collision while driving a Motorcycle.

WAIVER AND ASSUMPTION OF RISK

I, the reader, and/or purchaser of this book hereby acknowledge and understand that there are dangers and risks associated with the use, ownership, and the riding of a motorcycle.

I, the reader, and/or purchaser of this book, hereby voluntarily, at my own risk, by the act of reading and/or purchasing this book acknowledge that I have assumed the known risk associated with using, owning, and riding a motorcycle.

By reading and/or purchasing this book, I, the reader, and/or purchaser of this book, fully assume the dangers and risks, and agree to use my best judgment while engaging in those activities. I further agree to indemnify and hold harmless Robert Jaron, the author, his agents, licensees, successors, and assigns, from and against any and all liability incurred as a result of or in any manner related to my participation in the activities.

I, the reader and/or purchaser of this book, hereby fully waive and release Robert Jaron, the author, their contributors, agents, licensees, successors and assigns, from any and all claims for personal injury, property damage, or death that may result from my participation in the activity of using, owning, and riding a motorcycle.

I hereby certify that I am of legal age and competent to assume this implied waiver and assumption of risk, that in doing so of my own free will and accord, voluntarily and without duress, and that I do so intending to bind myself, my executor, my heirs, and administrators or assigns to the fullest extent.

By reading and/or purchasing this book, I have implicitly read and understood the foregoing, and acknowledge my consent to the terms of this waiver and assumption of Risk.

Table of Contents

Table of Illustrations 8

Preface 9

The 9 Primary Components 16

Chapter 1: Introduction 18

Chapter 2: Strategy 30

Chapter 3: Manage Your 4 Zones 42

Chapter 4: Create Space & Time........................... 71

Chapter 5: Expect the Unexpected 85

Chapter 6: Master the Use of Your Machine and Gear 103

Chapter 7: Be Alert, Engaged, and Scan for Potential Hazards 120

Chapter 8: Continue to Learn and Practice 123

Chapter 9: Conclusion: 128

The 9 Essential Concepts Revisited 132

Table of Illustrations

Figure 1: 4 Zones   43

Figure 2: Front Zone   45

Figure 3: Left Wall   59

Figure 4: Right Wall   62

Figure 5: Sleeper Hazard   66

Figure 6: Blind Hill   93

Figure 7: The 9 Medallion   132

Preface

Regardless of whether you're a new rider or an experienced one, this manual will provoke you to at least think about, and hopefully implement, a safer driving perspective and behavior, due to some sound ideas.

Let me begin, by explaining what motivated me to create and write this manual.

In a matter of a couple of years of riding a motorcycle, I developed some level of skill and confidence. I commuted often to work on the bike, went on many weekend short day rides, and overnight ones.

I read some and took some motorcycle driving-safety courses (3 of them); I chatted with friends and new acquaintances, and practiced. After those first couple of years, and 20,000 +/- miles, with no accidents, I was actually feeling a bit cocky! **Unjustifiably** so I might add.

Then one morning at a Diner, sitting down after a ride with a 'Breakfast Club,' I listened to a unique rider's story. He wasn't just anyone. This guy was a retired motorcycle police officer to boot. And with over 30+ years of professional and recreational riding experience under his belt. He got **all** my attention.

Why?

For me, this guy represented a motorcycle driver who was as good as you can get in regard to professional training, expertise, vast experience, maturity, and confidence.

What floored me was his story of when he experienced his first accident ***after*** all those decades of riding! That's right, after he had ridden all that time and retired from the police force as a motorcycle cop, he had his very first accident!

He told the story of how his wife was riding as a passenger with him one morning.

They were struck in an intersection by a vehicle that 'T-boned' them. They were injured to the extent that bones were broken and even an eye was lost. Thankfully no one died.

I am leaving out details because...it does not matter regarding the profound lesson I learned. And that lesson is:

"No matter how well I master my motorcycle,

and no matter how many miles & years I drive, shit can happen to even the best of drivers. *REGARDLESS OF WHO'S AT FAULT!* **And anyone, drivers and passengers included, can become victims of an accident in an instant.** "

Immediately after, I pondered long about my future as a motorcycle rider. I considered the following thoughts:

"Will the aftermath of an inevitable human error, regardless of whose fault, put me in harm's way also?"

"Is good 'luck' a real viable variable in motorcycle driving?"

And finally, "Is it just a matter of time before I too fall victim to a rendezvous with disaster?"

Though I had heard about other accidents, this particular story was **my** wake-up call! I loved riding, and I did not wish to end my romance with it. So, I began to think of how I could become more focused on **MY** motorcycle driving *safety*.

I wanted to help myself *reduce my risk* while driving, and hopefully improve my odds. And, out of fear, I became very determined of eliminating the experience of a motorcycle accident completely!

Though likely impossible, I decided it was certainly worth striving for!

It occurred to me that if I continued to listen to stories from others, I didn't need to experience an accident first hand to actually learn about them. So, I continued to listen intently.

The many close calls and accidents I heard about resulted in vehicle damage, bodily injuries, and hospitalizations. And sadly, some were about family, friends, or acquaintances that actually died.

This new enlightenment inspired me to adjust my focus, improve my state of mind, and began to create a work in process **strategy**.

Since that day, 14+ years, 140,000+ miles of driving with no accidents, and with a great deal of **thought and focus**, I created a **comprehensive strategy** resulting in a better-way for me. It's a **common sense approach strategy** that is designed to be exceptionally simple yet very affective.

I created what I call a: '***Motorcycle Driving Methodology & Risk- Ratio-Reduction Strategy'***. It is simple, logical, focused, and constructive.

The title: ***Arrive Alive without Incident***

pinpoints the primary context.

My strategy's **base focus is on the *benefits* of**

striving* to avoid <u>ALL</u> the *potential incidents that can

occur on the road.

I believe that **risk reduction** begins by

eliminating the **minor and major *close calls.*** Because

they are in essence the ***match and gunpowder*** of most

potential disasters waiting to happen! And in the

process, I developed a better and safer attitude,

enhanced my survivor driving skills and instincts, and

developed a real ***strategy*** that ***anyone*** can benefit from.

The 9 Primary Components

The following are a list of my 9 primary concepts, ideas, and key components that are the **foundation** to my methodology and *risk reduction strategy* that I am suggesting you embrace.

1. Embrace the concept of a *risk-ratio reduction strategy*.

2. Learn how to manage your **4 zones.**

3. Understand why *space and time* are relevant to driving safely.

4. Learn to *anticipate* well and *expect the*

unexpected.

    5. Embrace the concept of *lane-management.*

    6. Accept the concept of *sharing the road.*

    7. You should be *instinctively aware of the much greater risk* while driving a motorcycle vs. an automobile.

    8. Become more *focused on your well-being.*

    9. Develop the concept, discipline, and benefit of *self-critical analysis and self-teaching.*

Chapter 1: Introduction

A good constructive start is to put you in a basic driving scenario and review the options.

Basic situation:

You are driving your motorcycle, and you're planning on driving on a State Highway or Interstate Freeway.

You are approaching the beginning of the on-ramp to the Highway/Freeway. The on-ramp clearly has two lanes. While driving in the left lane, a vehicle is nose to nose with you in the right lane seeking to merge on the same road ahead. And up ahead, as on most Highway/Freeway on-ramps, this one narrows down to a single lane before allowing a vehicle to merge.

Concerning your immediate predicament, what would you do?

1-   Maintain matching acceleration speed as vehicle on right, ignore the situation, and stay on a possible collision with this motor vehicle?

2-   Slow down and bow-out to the vehicle on your right, allowing them the front position?

3-   Accelerate and move quickly forward of the vehicle to your right, (while not exceeding the speed limit), and safely take front position in the single merging lane on-ramp?

First off, in my opinion, option #1 is the only bad choice under any circumstance. You're obviously not paying attention and concerned about your well-being.

Option #2 is your conservative, safe, and best

response. And possibly, #2 is the only best response depending on many other possible variables.

#3 is a perfectly good final option if: You're fully engaged, very familiar with your machines acceleration and proficient in engaging it, anticipating the maneuver option in advance, and you can execute the move safely, swiftly, and with confidence while not exceeding the speed limit.

However, it certainly is no race to get on the darn roadway, right? So by all means, bow-out if the other vehicle has the same intention.

The point I am making with this simple scenario is, we do indeed have many options while driving and all are related to our attitude, behavior, concern for safety, our skill-set, and a whole lot more! And the dangers of riding a motorcycle on our public roadways should be obvious. But for many, it is not.

The following statistics from the National Highway Traffic Administration (NHTA), presents the following statistical FACTS concerning Motorcycles to embrace reality

The bottom line, and the point of sharing this data is to convince you of the REAL DANGER and DEADLY RISK associated with driving a motorcycle.

You don't have to take my word for it! Just continue reading!

In 2012, 4,957 motorcyclists were killed in motor vehicle traffic crashes- an increase of 7 percent from the 4,630 motorcyclists killed in 2011.

There were 93,000 motorcyclists injured during 2012, a 15-percent increase from 81,000 in 2011.

In 2012, 2,624 of all motorcyclists (52%) involved in fatal crashes collided with another type of motor vehicle in transport. In two-vehicle crashes, 75 percent of the motorcyclists involved in motor vehicle traffic crashes collided with the vehicle in the front of them. Only 7 percent were struck in the rear.

In 2012, there were 2,317 two-vehicle fatal crashes involving a motorcycle and another type of vehicle. In 41 percent (953) of these crashes, the other vehicles were turning left while the motorcycles were going straight, passing, or

overtaking other vehicles. Both

vehicles were going straight in 524

crashes (23%).

(Compliments of the NHTSA/ National Highway Transportation Safety Administration)

June 2014 NHTSA: National Highway Traffic Safety Administration. DOT HS 812 035

NHTSA'S National Center for Statistics and Analysis

http://www-rd.nhtsa.dot.gov/Pubs/812035.pdf)

A lot of thought provoking data is there people.

I suggest you review it again and read more on the

NHTSA website. Realize that the stats mostly cover

fatalities. And if you did not catch this tidbit, know this

now:

Statistically, the NHTSA data shows:

'In 2011 as a rider you were 30 times more likely than a passenger car occupant to die in a motor vehicle traffic crash and five times more likely to be injured while out riding a motorcycle.'

So wake up people!

This motorcycle riding we love to do, or are considering embarking on, is very dangerous indeed. The facts don't lie. You need more convincing...just look up 'motorcycle deaths' on Google and you will find thousands of results!

Or, go on You-Tube and look up 'motorcycle accidents'.

Both will certainly give you plenty of horrible reading and video material to convince you of how dangerous this method of travel is and how truly vulnerable we are.

And, we can all agree that driving a four-wheel vehicle, compared to a motorcycle, is safer by design.

Obvious considerations include four tires providing better traction and stability, seats and seat belts, steal cages, fenders, bumpers, windshield with wipers, likely better night time lighting, air bags, greater comfort, etc., and so forth.

Now, driving a motorcycle...well, having only two wheels and really no protection at all, except hopefully a helmet, an appropriate jacket, gloves, shoes, and pants, obviously puts us at a much greater risk! ***And we should be <u>instinctively aware</u> of that!***

However, based on observation of driving

behaviors, it appears that large portions of motorcycle drivers are NOT instinctively aware or even concerned at all! Certainly, the consequences of poor motorcycle driving are sometimes costly, painful, and deadly.

But based on observation, I ask the question: *'Why do so many motorcyclists drive with disregard for common sense safety concerns and* drive in a manner that appears that ***the actual laws of the road don't apply to them!***

You know whom I'm talking about. Perhaps it is you? I have to admit, I too have succumbed to this behavior at times, but it is in my past.

The wind-in-our-hair feeling, the freedom, exhilaration, etc., etc., **all can intoxicate us from the reality of extreme danger and consequence.** But the facts are clear. Motorcycle riding is a far more dangerous method of travel than driving a car or other options we have.

New or experienced riders, ask your selves the following questions:

Do you find that other motor vehicle drivers are cutting you off?

Do you think of all other vehicle drivers as the enemy or as jerks?

Do you have close calls frequently or rarely?

Do you split lanes in traffic at high speeds, exceeding the posted speed limit?

Do you tailgate?

Are you constantly weaving between cars?

Do you drive, feeling that only good luck will truly keep you safe?

While driving a motorcycle, are you day dreaming and not focused on your well-being and the constant danger?

The Purpose of This Manual:

Develop a sound driving attitude and a beneficial *risk-ratio-reduction strategy* regardless of your experience.

Embrace an easy-to-learn driving strategy that will encourage and enable you to drive more safely immediately.

Learn about a logical approach to *zone-defense* **driving** that will simplify the task.

Understand why space and time are relevant to

driving safety.

Learn how **_lane-management_** will help you **reduce your _risk-ratio_**.

Heighten your awareness of valuable statistics.

Discover the importance of being proficient in the operation of your motorcycle and gear.

Experience more clarity on what to focus on, one ride at a time.

Lastly, learn more on how you can proactively modify your current driving state of mind, behavior, and focus, and... **_strive_** to now **Arrive _Alive Without Incident_**!

Do you first need to have a bad accident to pique your interest in all this? It didn't for me

.

Chapter 2: Strategy

There are four primary components, or building blocks, to what I call my, *'Risk-Ratio-Reduction Strategy'*:

-**Attitude**

- **Incident Awareness**

- **Strategy**

- **Self-Critical Analysis and Teaching**

All are essential to understand my empowering defensive motorcycle driving approach. Let's begin.

1. Attitude

Wikipedia defines the word *attitude* as

> *'A favorable or unfavorable evaluation of something. Attitudes are generally positive or negative views of a*

person, place, thing, or event—this is often referred to as the attitude object. People can also be conflicted or ambivalent toward an object, meaning that they simultaneously possess both positive and negative attitudes toward the item in question.'

Here is what I consider an example of a sound and mature attitude as a safety concerned Motorcyclist:

"I love to ride, yet I am very concerned about the dangers associated with motorcycle driving. I keep in mind that driving any motor vehicle is a privilege the governing state extends to others and me. And abiding by the law, sharing the road, striving to driving well and safe, and setting a good example, are all safer and sound ideas.

I embrace the fact that driving a motorcycle is especially dangerous and challenging compared to driving a car. And knowing that, I continue to learn and practice.

When I drive, I am rested and fully engaged in the task at hand. When needed, I will take a break while on a drive, and I certainly will not consume any alcohol or drugs that will diminish my driving abilities.

Last but not least, I put aside mental issues that might take my mind off my 'A' game. I am engaged, focused, and embrace the challenge of driving a motorcycle." (RJ)

That is **my** attitude, **and I think has many sound valid components.**

I strongly suggest you *embrace all of the*

rationale, and perhaps create a better one that works for you!

The bottom line is we all need to be more focused on our safety!

And, it starts with a **sound attitude.** What's yours?

2. Incident Awareness

Webster's Dictionary defines the word **incident** as:

> *'That which falls out or takes place; an event; casualty, occurrence. Adj.: incident—falling or striking on something.'*

Here are some minor and major examples of motor vehicle driving 'incidents':

Hearing a horn sound from another driver

Getting cut off or you cutting someone off

Experiencing a close-call lane change

Not experiencing a smooth and well-anticipated vehicle lane merge on or off a highway/freeway ramp

Experiencing an incident at an intersection

Swerving and/or braking hard

Running a yellow or red light

Rolling through a stop sign

Experiencing a right-of-way incident

Nearly hitting a vehicle from behind

Getting in any accident with a motor vehicle or any stationary object

Dropping one's motorcycle

Having a problem in a parking lot

Taking a curve too wide or too fast

Being unprepared for weather

Not adequately checking your machine (examples: running out of gas, experiencing avoidable mechanical breakdown)

Getting a traffic ticket

Not anticipating things popping out at you: vehicles, pedestrians, animals, etc., etc.

Tire slippage due to weather condition

Tire slippage due to road debris

Hundreds, if not thousands of incident examples can be made. We all experience them. And as I mentioned before, I believe that *risk-reduction begins* *by eliminating the minor incidents as wells as the major 'close-calls'.*

Common sense and logic will support that any incident that first appears to be minor at review, could indeed had been the catalyst of a major disaster!

3. Strategy:

Wikipedia defines the word *strategy* as

> *'A **plan of action** designed to achieve a vision. It derives from the Greek strategia 'office of general, command, generalship.'*

Plan of Action:

The title: **Arrive Alive Without Incident** (AAWI) is the *vision of my strategy.*

The primary focus of this plan of action is to

reduce our risk, moment to moment, ***one ride at a time!***

What's that saying: 'Live in the Moment'?

Well concerning motorcycle driving, I suggest you **'Drive-in-the-Moment.'**

Be focused in the present. And like learning any task, breaking the task in small increments is a sound idea.

Examples:

How about focusing on keeping yourself, and perhaps a passenger, un-scathed on this busy Freeway ***right now?***

How about, driving safely in this rain, or in the darkness of night?

Or, focus on your safety now till the next gas stop or next town.

Or simply, get to work with no incident safe & sound!

Don't think too far ahead. Instead, ***drive-in-the-moment*** and be focusing and striving to achieve an ***incident-free-ride from point A to point B!***

Why? Because, every incident can result in a potential accident of course! Once again, driving a motorcycle ***is*** more challenging and dangerous than driving a car. And if you're not wanting anymore of those challenges in your life, I suggest you ***not*** drive a motorcycle!

4. Self-Critical Analysis and Teaching

Concerning all incidents, regardless of who was at fault, the question ***I suggest you ask yourself*** is this:

'What could I have done to better **anticipate** that incident?'

And better yet, ***'How could I have better anticipated that situation and avoided the incident entirely?'***

The enlightenment you'll receive from ***self-critical analysis and self-teaching,*** is a critical part of this strategy. When we learn from each motorcycle incident, we can ***train ourselves*** to anticipate each of them the next time!

I strongly urge you to think long and hard about this.

Whether you're a novice or advanced rider, through this incident analysis thought process, if you are honest with yourself, you will find that most of the time you could have **avoided** that incident entirely.

And placing or seeking fault, and playing a blame-game, is unconstructive and a waste of time.

That game will eventually get us all hurt or killed out there.

I urge you to break that habit immediately. *Lose the anger and the blame.*

A near miss is perhaps a lucky outcome indeed, but I have avoided many near misses by simply *anticipating* them. And I am sure that some of the advanced riders, who are mentally focused on their well-being, do the same.

The obvious critical need is to learn from each experience/incident.

Than by recall, due to previous analysis, you will

start to instinctively, anticipate them as I have. And with this *focused awareness*, you will likely avoid many potential incidents on the road, and hopefully, with some luck—all of them.

The next and more advanced step is to use your imagination combined with your experience and knowledge. This will empower yourself to truly *expect the unexpected* while driving! Think of it like playing the game of Chess. Can we envision the possible 'moves' of our opponents out on the road? I think we can. This will be discussed later on in this manual.

Chapter 3: Manage Your 4 Zones

I wish to introduce what I call, **'Zone Defense Driving'**. With so many changing variables, and so many potential dangers 360 degrees around us, the task at hand is huge. If we break the road environment down into four zones, this will simplify the task of driving a motorcycle and, it will enable you to focus more intensely and efficiently.

What are the four zones?

1-Front Zone

2-Rear Zone

3-Left Zone

4-Right Zone

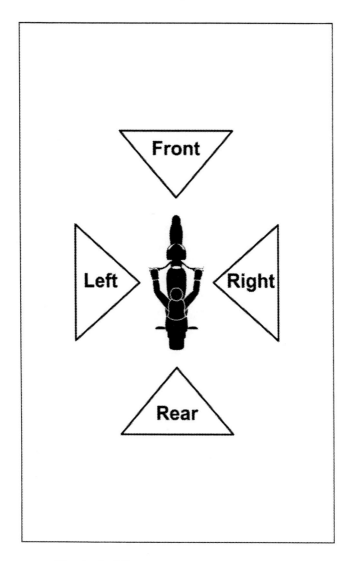

Figure 1: **4 Zones**

1-Front Zone

Tailgating a vehicle in front of you is probably the **most frequent and stupidest thing** most drivers do. Don't ever tailgate on a motorcycle. You're not going to get anywhere sooner by tailgating someone. And on a motorcycle, it's insane.

Any impact, even at slow speeds, will delay your journey, cause unnecessary damage to your bike, and perhaps even to you. And at moderately high speeds, I have heard of drivers being ejected in the air off their bikes, and onto or over the vehicle they rear-ended.

Whatever the case, you should shake this habit immediately. You have no time to react. *Tailgating is an accident waiting to happen. End it!*

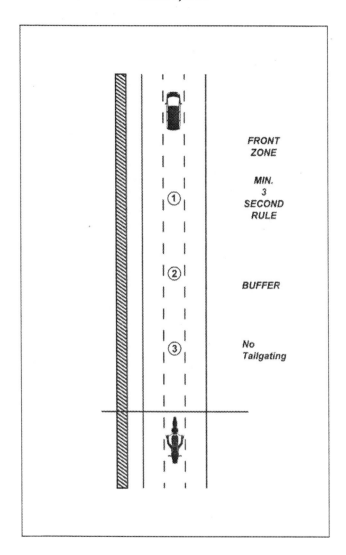

Figure 2: **Front Zone**

If you're not tailgating and are following the **minimum 2-3second rule of space**, behind a motor vehicle, then you have created a **safer** front zone. (The rule for California is 3 seconds.) [Ref: 2014 California DMV motorcycle manual.]

If you are being tailgated, slow down safely and create **additional** space in the front zone. Consider changing lanes and allow the motorist to pass you. Then move back into your chosen lane.

The most important thing to remember is ***don't be pressured to tailgate.*** Hold your ground and move on your terms.

(If you recall from your basic DMV readings, the minimum non-tailgating rule applies ***only to dry roads in daylight hours***. Keep that in mind while you are managing your front space zone.]

And while driving in your safer front zone, look farther ahead than the immediate car in front of you. Look through windshields, above and around vehicles— *scan for hazards and signals, or clues of any kind*.

Examples of Visual Clues:

Red glowing break lights, turn signals, swerving vehicles, lane-changing patterns, road signs, approaching exits and on-ramps, merging and exiting vehicles regarding those ramps, intersections, new weather and road conditions, pedestrians, children at play, dogs, blind corners, hills, or alleys, and so forth.

And besides **visually** observing, **listen** for the following:

Screeching tires, wailing sirens, blaring horns, the sounds of vehicle impacts, and such. The valuable clues you can *see and hear* are endless.

Seeking out or scanning for all clues will allow you to manage your immediate driving status appropriately if your engaged, focused, and paying attention.

And if you are not actually *anticipating* what motorists do, then this is the time to introduce this important concept. Based on all your previous driving experiences while driving a car, *predict what drivers can possibly choose to do and act on that knowledge!*

Tailgaters:

It's also important to be aware of the tailgaters **around** you.

You will find that those tailgating near you, on the front or the sides, will be **more likely to change**

lanes and cut you off. As car drivers, we witness this all the time.

And much of the time, these lane changes occur without any turn signal or warning. In addition, these tailgaters around you are most likely to **rear-end** the vehicle in front of them!

So when driving, **I personally focus with extreme caution on ALL tailgating.**

If I am approaching a tailgater on my right or left, I try to avoid the likely and abrupt cut-off or lane change.

I anticipate this by knowing what occupies my left, right, and front zones. And much of the time, I change lanes to avoid the potential incident entirely.

Or if I am traveling in the far left 'Fast Lane', and

have plenty of space in my front zone, I anticipate the tailgaters to my right, and his possible cut-off move. I immediately move to the far LEFT position in my lane, and swiftly accelerate while tapping my horn. Clearing the Right Zone cut-off hazard altogether.

Or, I can choose to simply slow down and allow the anticipated cut-off lane change to occur. Just let it go.

Arrive alive without incident, right?

*Having options **by creating more space and time** is always ideal and beneficial.*

(I will discuss more about lane choice consideration and in-lane positioning options later).

Common Sense and Maturity:

No matter what your present state of mind is,

your default should always be focused on your personal well-being. *So slowing down, bowing-out, allowing egress, being courteous, and sharing the road... is ALWAYS the best and safest move.*

Just remember, you're not in the safe enclosure of a car. So evaluate the risk and remember that your #1 mission now is: **Arrive Alive Without Incident! (AAWI)**

Front Zone Conclusion:

If you maintain and manage the front zone well, you will have successfully engaged in the beginning of a **Risk-Ratio Reduction Strategy.** (RRRS)

And again, remember that the zones around you extend **way beyond what you can see and hear.** *Scanning* and expanding your scope as far as you can is essential. And realize that just because you don't see or hear it, doesn't mean the hazard does not exist.

2-Rear Zone

Rear-End collisions on our roadways happen very frequently. So, getting rear-ended on a motorcycle is a very possible reality. So if you're being **tailgated**, *slow down safely and increase the space in front of you.* And even consider changing lanes and allowing the vehicle behind you to pass. After, just smoothly, and safely move right back in your chosen lane. When you are driving in a lot of traffic, depending on the severity and attitude of the tailgater behind you, perhaps go with the flow and hold your ground.

Again, **don't let drivers pressure you** to tailgate and speed if you don't want to.

Also, as a general rule of thumb, if you are stopped for any reason, such as while waiting for a light to turn green, at a stop sign, or stuck in commute traffic, **have an 'out' path**. You perhaps can move to the left or right to avoid a rear-end collision. Realize though, to enable you to do this quick enough, *get in the habit of keeping your bike in-gear when you are stopped.*

In a pinch, this step could allow you to move in that instant and avoid being hit from behind. This is a great example of grasping the principle to *expect the unexpected* to occur.

Also, don't forget about motorcycle **lane splitters** approaching you from behind and passing you. In California, most **'Lane Sharing'**, as it is called, usually occurs in between the very far Left 'Fast Lane', and the immediate lane to the right. If you're traveling in the far left lane, and you're NOT splitting lanes, choose to be in **the far left side** position of the 'fast lane'. This allows motorcyclist to easily pass you on your **right** while they are sharing the lane.

And when you stop at any intersection, anticipate motorcyclists who split lanes to get to the front of the stopped traffic.

(More on **Lane Management** later.)

This subject however is a good example of an old yet sound driving concept called: **'Share the Road'**. Yes, other motorcyclists are sharing the road with you too. And I suggest you be courteous and more aware of ALL the different types of motor vehicles we share the road with.

A great example is say "Hello" to all those Big-Rig Commercial Vehicles, Construction Trucks, and open Pick-Up Trucks on our roadways! They are everywhere in America. I personally stay clear of these vehicles when riding my motorcycle.

I expect the unexpected of them cutting me off, suddenly throwing off one of those commercial re-cap tire pieces, or just dropping debris in my path!

They want to change lanes in front of you, let them! Drivers in general claim they do not see us before most accidents occur on the road. So, slow down, share the road, anticipate, and move away safely on your terms.

Rear Zone Conclusion:

If you're paying attention to those in front and

behind you, actively **managing** your rear and front zones, creating more **space**, and seeking an alternate 'out' **path**, you will likely have a better chance of avoiding front and rear collisions.

You achieve this by **creating** a combined larger front and backspace or buffer, to allow you more **space and time** to take action more safely.

By actively managing the space you occupy at all times will further enhance your awareness and again simplify the task of driving a motorcycle.

3-Left Zone:

Watch for cars in your Left Zone extensively while you merge to any space in the left side/zone.

Obviously, vehicles may likely want to merge to their right at the same time.

Beware!

Get in the habit of looking in side mirrors and over your shoulders when merging any lanes.

Share the road and allow smooth safe merges to occur for all engaging motor vehicles, by accelerating smoothly and safely or braking if need be.

This Left Zone is to be managed equally well as all your other zones.

Back-To-The-Wall:

One major beneficial suggestion I have to share, that I do religiously while driving is, when I enter a multi-lane highway or freeway, *I safely move to the far-left lane ASAP!* Again, we often refer to this lane as the '**fast-lane**'.

When you're driving in the far-left lane on any

divided roadway, it is very **less** likely for vehicles to move into your lane from your *left side/Zone.* And when a barrier, such as a guardrail or concrete divider, divides the roadway and virtually safe guards our Left Zone, think of this unique moment as having your **back-to-the-wall.**

In theory, the **left side** of you is against the wall, so to speak. This concept is another example of the *risk-ratio reduction strategy* that I am introducing.

By taking advantage of this approach of putting your **left zone to-the-wall**, you can focus more on your other three zones: Front/Rear/Right.

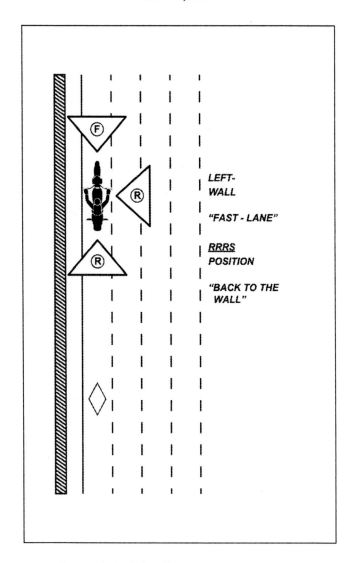

LEFT-
WALL

"FAST - LANE"

RRRS
POSITION

"BACK TO THE
WALL"

Figure 3: **Left Wall**

Exception Warning:

Though rare, vehicles on the opposite side of a divided road, even with concrete walls or metal dividers separating us, can be **breached** by vehicles. And divided roadways with nothing more than landscaping, such as grass and brush, sometimes do little or nothing to protect you. And finally, we of course have periodic openings in our divided 'wall' of protection, allowing intersecting roadways and vehicles to enter our lane from the left side. So just, keep all that in mind.

But regardless of the exceptions, when in this far left 'fast' lane, on a divided roadway, we do indeed have a great benefit!

More time and energy to fine-tune our focus in zones with a higher probability of danger is huge! And that is why I think the l**eft side fast lane is the safest**

and smartest place to be on a multi-lane divided roadway while driving a motorcycle.

Comment:

Additional Benefit of this back-to-the-wall benefit is that it is sometimes available on our RIGHT SIDE as well! To be clear, I am NOT suggesting you drive in the far right lane frequently. [*The far right lane is only for merging on and off any roadway.*]

However, back to the point, the exception of when the ***back-to-the-wall benefit*** is available in the **far right lane** is noted in the following picture.

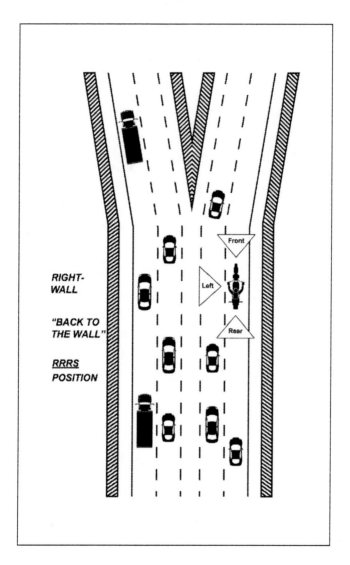

Figure 4: **Right Wall**

All highways, freeways, turnpikes have intersecting roadways. Examples in my area are State Highways 101 and 280 north bound.

While traveling north on 101 highway, 280 branches off ahead on the **RIGHT SIDE**. There are actually two lanes for the 280 branching off. The **risk-reduction** benefit here is to anticipate the merge you wish to do to your right, from one roadway to another early, and *move to the far right lane, near the wall.*

This way you are in the far right lane, *anticipating* all the vehicles merging to the RIGHT also which are now on your LEFT side/zone. And again, having the 'wall' on your right side in this instance, you will reduce your *risk-ratio* in the RIGHT ZONE and allow you to focus more on vehicles in your Front, Rear, and now LEFT ZONE.

Last but not least, you will have the right

shoulder as an out-path if need be. This ***back-to-the-wall*** concept has the same obvious defensive benefits as

when on the far left side. A Great new Strategy tool!

[Recall Figure 4]

Middle Lane Choice:

Now when needing/choosing to drive in any

middle lane, (vehicles on your left and right), you are

vulnerable in your **left and right zones.** So, you will

need to proactively evaluate and observe vehicles in

both zones *simultaneously.*

Another thought of importance concerning your

L**eft Zone** while in a middle lane, or Right Zone for that

matter, is to be especially focused when ***you're***

approaching an exit **ahead.**

Scan your left zone and ***anticipate vehicles intending on exiting*** the roadway or turning right at the next intersection. Anticipate this. And watch for last-second ***Exit-Jumpers*** or '***Sleeper'*** drivers!

You know those vehicles that swoop across multiple lanes and aim for the upcoming exit. Beware of these sleepy dangerous drivers! **This is another good reason I highly recommend you avoid driving in any far-right 'slow' lane unless you're getting off at the next *immediate* exit.** You're a moving target for those exit-jumpers. Anticipate this folks!

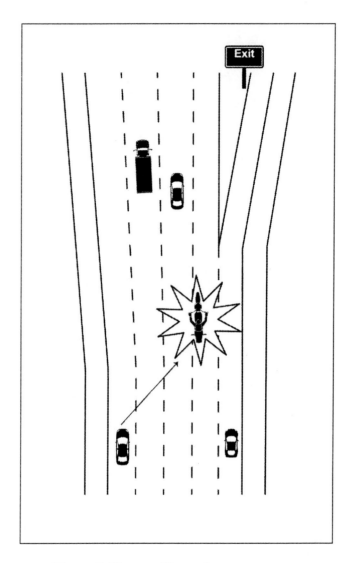

Figure 5: **Sleeper Hazard**

Left Zone Conclusion:

If you're successfully managing your front, back, and left zones on any roadway as I suggest, you are now engaging in a 'multiple zone risk-ratio-reduction strategy' state of mind.

And if you're beginning to recall your personal incident experience history, you will indeed continue to further reduce your risk-ratio factor. That is the precise intention!

4-Right Zone:

Regarding your left zone, watch for vehicles that are merging and approaching you in your **right** zone equally well. As previously noted, watch for tailgaters. And of course, **stay out of driver's blind spots in either side Zones.**

When you pass highway exits anticipate vehicles merging onto the roadway on your Right side/Right Zone immediately after the EXIT as well! This is a no-brainer folks! The frequent occurrence of merging vehicles in the right lane is very predictable! So act on this knowledge, and further reduce your risk by reducing your time in the far right lane.

Also, use the middle lanes as **in-frequently** as possible! You do have a safer choice that I strongly suggested if you now recall. Again, by choosing to drive mostly in any **FAR LEFT 'FAST LANE' of a divided roadway**, you will immediately *reduce your risk* by eliminating the **Left Zone** as an **equal** concern as other zones.

Right Zone Conclusion:

Like all zones, while driving; be scanning your

right zone extensively.

Watch for predictable behaviors, such as tailgaters, constant blind spot occupancy issues, exits, and merging and exiting ramps, and act on that knowledge.

Remember that anticipating and being courteous are sound concepts to consider! Allow people to merge into your left or right zones. Mature and evolve as a motorcycle driver and embrace the concept of *sharing the road!* You'll likely live longer.

Chapter Conclusion:

Finally, if you successfully **manage** your front, back, left, and right zones well, you are fully engaging in a *Risk-Ratio-Reduction Strategy. (RRRS)*

Now, truly eliminating all risk while driving a

motorcycle is impossible. But this 'Zone Defense' or four-zone focus, will make the task of driving a motorcycle more manageable as I intended.

Think of managing all four zones as spinning and balancing fragile china plates on sticks while riding a unicycle.

It's no easy task, but I find challenging and actually fun. It will also keep you keenly engaged and alert!

Chapter 4: Create Space & Time

Creating more *space*, and thereby creating more *time* while driving, benefits us all tremendously. This is especially critical while driving a motorcycle.

As an example, creating more space when you're **not tailgating** provides you with more time to react, slow down, and stop safely when need be. And keep in mind that an *acceleration of speed* will have the *opposite* effect, and *reduce* that space and reaction time factor instantaneously! So, **just by slowing down, you will create a safer buffer of space and time** *immediately.*

Let's break it down.

1. Space:

Wikipedia defines *space* as

> *'The boundless, three-dimensional*
> *extent in which objects and events occur*
> *and have relative position and direction'*

Well, this definition of space certainly relates to driving. And in this case, more space provides us the opportunity to be more relaxed and focused on the task of driving, while creating more time to react and take appropriate action when need be.

Lane Management:

*In-Lane Position **Space** Management:*

I previously shared my suggestions on which lanes to drive in and why. Now, after choosing a lane, should we: drive stationary in the *center, left or right* of the lane?

Lane-position options have many schools of thought that are certainly debatable.

Here are the most memorable I can recall. The idea that *moving around* within a lane you occupy provokes drivers to *see you* better. This may be helpful but I think if being seen is your concern, just **wear bright colored clothing** for starters.

Another comment I have read concerns avoiding the middle of a lane due to a possible slick oil trail left by vehicles. This would be valid perhaps 50+ years ago when cars would drip enough oil on the road too constitute a road hazard. However, as for **parking lots**, oil **& radiator fluid** are real present-day dangers.

Now back to the middle of the road, due to the right and left sides of all lanes being most *tire-traveled*, there is a real possibility of **debris, gravel, and sand** present! So beware of that hazard!

But concerning our limited space and time, I would *be* **most concerned with our primary imminent deadly threat,** other MOTOR VEHICLES!

Creating additional space, by choosing a more **advantageous defensive in-lane position** is valuable because it will provide you with critical vehicle avoidance and maneuvering space and time.

Example:

Where will you go when those right zone tailgater's change lanes into the left lane you occupy?

If you are not tailgating and, on-guard/ready, you like me, can easily **accelerate FORWARD and LEFT** or, choose to **brake/slow down and move BACK and**

LEFT, in your lane.

(If you have a tailgater behind *you, at the same time*, the FORWARD OPTION IS YOUR ONLY SAFE OPTION to avoid a rear-end collision) And realize the front **forward and Left** move is available only IF YOU CREATED THE AMPLE SPACE in your Front Zone!

Are you beginning to see how the management of Zones and our In-Lane Position choices can be **choreographed** to your advantage now?

Generally speaking, when driving in the *center position of any lane*, you will be in the most *neutral space* when vehicles are on your left and right sides.

Read on to see the value of creating more space between you and your most imminent threat!

Lane Splitting/Sharing Space:

This topic of Lane Splitting/Sharing Space could be brought up in a variety of chapters in this book. I however wish to bring up again now because of its extreme danger directly related to *Space and Time, and Lane Management.* **In California Lane Sharing is legal. Yet, I do so very rarely due to my priority being *risk-reduction.***

Here are some concerns:

Just because you CAN split/share lanes, you ***don't have to do it!*** And if you choose to, you can ***create your own rules of engagement of when and how!***

Also, if legal for you, splitting lanes will bring you into peoples' left and right ***blind spots*** on a constant car-to-car basis!

Think about it. You will be approaching EVERY car's blind spot as you approach from the rear. So... BEWARE!

I have read many motorcyclists actually claim that driving a motorcycle is **safer while** splitting lanes than **not** doing so. You can read all about the controversy or debate on the Internet. Be it fact or fiction, lane splitting, **is a personal choice! And**, I wish to emphasize, a choice you can make on a **per-ride basis**. Ask yourself, "*Is the risk necessary today or perhaps right now?*"

Here are some variables to consider:

Would you split lanes with a passenger on board?

At what speed do other vehicles need to be

going for you to discontinue doing it? 25, 30, 55MPH?

Would you split lanes while exceeding the posted speed limit?

Would you split lanes in the rain or at night?

Would you split lanes on a rough or narrow road?

How about during rush hour, or commute traffic?

Are you feeling well at this moment? Are other concerns on my mind taking me away from my *A-Game* while driving?

While I'm not totally against it, I do it rarely and I have set my terms of not exceeding 30/35 MPH while doing it. I don't feel comfortable combing a higher rate of speed with the obvious additional risk. Try it yourself if/where permitted. How does it feel to you? Simply stated, my gut tells me, *"Beware and do it at your own risk!"*

Though I can predict a great deal out there on the road, I'm just very concerned about the **reduction** of critical space and time to do anything appropriate.

I'm always amazed to watch motorcyclists splitting lanes here in California traveling at 50-60+ MPH, while cars are barely moving. Many motorcyclists are even **exceeding** the posted speed limit while splitting lanes! This is certainly NOT **'safe'** driving. The question to ask yourself is this, is getting to your destination minutes sooner worth the risk? Weigh the risk factors and decide.

When I'm caught in a slow craw and choose **not**

to split lanes, that is when I practice my slow-driving balance skills, and relax. Also, increasing the front-zone space allows me to cruise at a constant speed without stopping.

Sharing the Road:

I can't overstate this point and its benefit. Because we interact with other drivers while sharing roads and lanes, it's important and beneficial to be mindful of how other drivers perceive us and perhaps develop a bad attitude toward all motorcycle drivers.

Being courteous, for example, will earn you some righteous respect by some. ***And sharing and obeying the same laws of the road, is <u>expected.</u>***

Irritating a driver may lead to immediate and dangerous repercussions. ('Road Rage') Let's do all we can to eliminate that, shall we?

Also, I suggest taking your emotions toward these other drivers out of the equation entirely. Simply anticipate their actions best you can, take action, and move-on (literally).

Blind Spot 'Space':

As you move past motor vehicles on your left and/or right, depending on what lane you are driving, be acutely aware of **YOU** occupying all blind-spot space **of other vehicles!** When driving in *congested commute traffic*, that is when blind spot occupancy will be compounded at *an **accelerated rate, non-stop**.*

And once again, observe how vehicles on either side may be tailgating also! When approaching tailgaters blind spot, say on your RIGHT, move to the LEFT SIDE OF YOUR LANE, assuming this tailgater is your most immediate threat, and SLOW DOWN. Or, move with extreme caution. ***Anticipate*** the quick lane changes into your lane!

2. Time:

A simple definition states that 'time is what clocks measure.'

For motorcycle drivers, creating more 'measure' (space) really means you create more time to react. In fact, simply rolling down the throttle and slowing down, could be your first plausible reaction to many situations.

Why? Because it gives you more space and ***time immediately.***

Speeding, as in driving beyond the posted speed limit, is something we all do often here in California

There's no question that driving fast is fun. I've

certainly gotten my share of speeding tickets.

However, speeding is not only illegal but also crazy to do at times. Speeding causes you to lose critical reaction *space and time* to do what is appropriate. There are way too many variables with causes and effects to name here.

Traffic congestion, evening hours, weather, carrying a passenger, etc., etc. Engage your brain, think rationally, and make sound decisions concerning your wellbeing and perhaps someone else's *in the present moment.*

Chapter Conclusion

Actively managing your *space and time* in an intelligent, logical, and keenly focused way gives you much-needed time to react to variables.

I think motorcycle riding requires a level of concentration and focused strategy.

It requires you to anticipate possible moves of your opponents, like in the game of Chess or a choreographed and practiced dance with the other vehicles.

And while driving on your motorcycle, every little bit of extra space will give you critical time to possibly save your ass. While occupying any lane, Center/Left/Right, micro-manage your lane position as an additional option you control.

Evaluate the risk characteristics of the vehicles immediately around you. And move freely to your left, middle, and right, as you occupy any lane... defensively.

Chapter 5: Expect the Unexpected

If we have our heads in the game, we certainly are ***anticipating the expected*** things to occur, such as drivers not using turn signals yet turning and changing lanes, or running a stop sign.

How about anticipating a rear end collision due to any vehicle tailgating?

Or, consider the possibility that there might be road debris or a wet road up ahead on a blind corner or blind hill? We can also be prepared and *expect* the abrupt crossing of a child, pedestrian, or dog on a residential street.

Yes, if we're fully engaged, we can and need to scan, process, and act on our common sense, knowledge, and experience as drivers for much of these **expected** things.

Now with so many common expected variables on the road to watch for, is it conceivable to ***add to our plates*** and also ***anticipate*** the ***unexpected*** to occur? I think so, and I strongly suggest you try.

I believe we can ***insightfully imagine and anticipate a great deal of unlikely unexpected*** things that might also occur.

Examples:

We ***can*** be prepared for the **unexpected** red-light runner by ***not*** jumping a green light and ***looking to the left before*** entering any intersection.

Can the possible sudden crossing of a deer when entering a Forest be anticipated?

Why not!

How about the **unexpected** car pulling out from a blind alley/driveway, or around a blind corner? Yes, we can!

And we can certainly imagine and anticipate the **unexpected** potential *head-on collision* of another motor vehicle that is now crossing into our lane when passing or *are approaching a blind corner or hill.*

We can also anticipate and make a habit of not driving beside a big-rig tracker trailer to avoid an **unexpected** re-cap tire to peel-off. Or not drive behind loaded open trucks to avoid any falling debris.

Yes, we can proactively *imagine* and *anticipate* many unlikely *unexpected* things out on these unsafe/dangerous roadways.

Worst Nightmares:

Now here are some examples of our ***worst nightmares*** out on the road while driving a motorcycle that might catch us all...off-guard.

Can we strategically expect the irrational behavior of a drunken, drug induced, or sleeping driver?

How about a reckless speeding driver who is being pursued by the Police in a chase?

Or, the unseen motor vehicle **behind** that is about to rear-end us or cause another vehicle to do so? And finally, how about a ***deliberate*** collision induced by another motor vehicle?

Sadly, perhaps we can and will ***fall victim*** to these ***extreme reckless or outrageous bizarre circumstances** that* are un-avoidable. God or luck may indeed play a role on these incident outcomes.

The bottom line point is this, ***driving a motorcycle is always dangerous*** and much more dangerous than driving ***IN a car.*** And some ***unexpected*** things can happen anytime under any circumstances.

Here are more examples of things you might or might not expect:

Drivers who take their eyes off the road to text or chat on cell phones, adjust the radio, or take a sip of coffee

Vehicles, such as motorcycles, can easily slip on gravel/sand or wet slippery surfaces, such as wet pavement, metal manhole covers, or railroad tracks.

An unexpected tire blowout on your motorcycle or on another vehicle could be very alarming and cause havoc.

A vehicle collision near you that inadvertently causes your vehicle to collide with a vehicle or object

The elderly or newly licensed drivers

The possibilities are endless. You still think driving a motorcycle is a good idea?

Blind Spots:

I discussed the relation of blind spots in the topic of Space and Time earlier.

But, here again, they are related to this chapter's subject: Expect the Unexpected, and it can't be over emphasized.

The issues of Blind Spots are constant while driving any motor vehicle and especially dangerous while on a motorcycle.

Again, on any roadway, not only are we constantly approaching or in 'blind spots' of other motor vehicles, but we are also approaching **blind spaces** such as blind corners, blind hills, alleys, parked cars, etc. on a never ending occurrence.

The question is, "Can we **expect the unexpected** so we successfully avoid a potential hazard concerning them all?" I think much of the time we can if we pro-actively create more space and time, soundly manage our lane choices, and our in-lane position options wisely.

Blind-Corners/Hill

(Head-On Collision Danger)

I drive the beautiful, coastal Highway 1 in the San Francisco Bay area. Much of this roadway consists of two lanes: one going north and the other going south. And much of the roadway has blind corners/hills. All undivided roadways are dangerous, not excluding the scenic ones! **So once again, beware!**

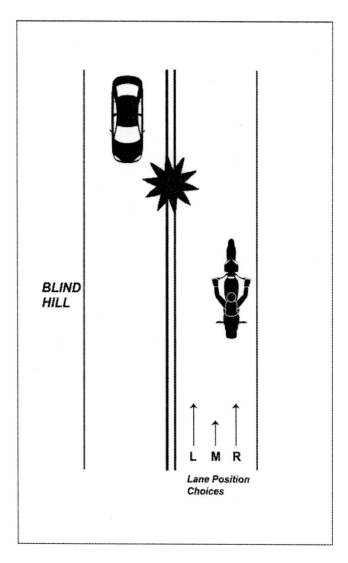

Figure 6: **Blind Hill**

In this example, I'm driving up the crest of a hill at the posted speed of fifty-five miles an hour, and I cannot see any possible approaching motor vehicle due to the ***blind- hill space.*** So, I choose to move to the ***center or right side*** of the lane.

Why?

Because many times, I have encountered a vehicle that comes toward me and has crossed the center painted line. Perhaps it is someone making a deliberate risky pass at a high rate of speed. Maybe it's just someone not paying attention and making a terrible error.

In any case, these drivers could potentially cause a ***head-on*** collision with me!

When I'm in the **center or right side of my**

lane and anticipate this possible threat, I hopefully have *space and time* to maneuver away.

However, if I were driving in the left side of the lane, I would be closer to that threat and would have less time to move over. This is another consideration concerning your Lane-Management options.

Intersections & Intersecting Roadways:

WARNING:

I have chosen to place this topic here, due to the statistically frequent occurrence of intersection motorcycle accidents.

Anyone can check on line to verify there are many sources that support this.

As an example, according to the NHTSA 2011 data, of the ' 2,449 (49%) of all fatal motorcycle crashes were the results of a bike colliding with another vehicle.'

A large percentage of them were the result of another vehicle turning left in front of the motorcycle that was either going straight, passing or overtaking another vehicle.'

Hello! When you approach any intersection, these areas should feel like you're going through an explosive mine field. And for God's sake...SLOW DOWN here! Be careful, anticipate, and expect the *un-expected* here.

Intersection Safety Tips:

Plan where you want to be going *before* you approach any intersection!

WATCH FOR APPROACHING FRONT ZONE VEHICLES AND ASSUME THEY WILL TURN IN FRONT

OF YOU!

Observe the intersection road condition for potentially slick metal or painted surfaces. (When you cross-slippery surfaces, counter balance your weight to enhance tire traction and prevent a fall.

Yield right-of-way to vehicles and pedestrians

SLOW DOWN

Don't ever run a red or yellow light.

Always **hesitate** and look to the left, right, and in front of you, before accelerating on a green light.

Watch for red light runners.

Don't do any illegal lane changes or turns in an intersection. (If you're about to miss a turn for whatever reason, go through the intersection and come back the other way safely.)

Avoid any incident. Don't take unnecessary risks while crossing any intersection.

While stopped at an intersection, leave your bike in gear and observe your rear zone. Have a way-out option if a rear end collision is imminent.

Residential and Business Roads:

Twenty-five and thirty-five miles per hour are the speed limits. Obey them. Drive carefully. Beware of intersections as noted prior. Watch your four zones and don't get too relaxed just because you're at a slow speed. Anticipate and expect the unexpected.

Examples:

Watch for cars backing out of driveways in your path!

On June 2014, in Redwood City California, a

fellow motorcycle driver DIED in a 25 MPH residential area, being hit by someone backing out of his or her driveway!

The reality is **we are always vulnerable** when driving a motorcycle, even at **slow** speeds!

Public Roadways vs. Racetracks:

Warning: *The public road is certainly not even close to a well-paved, smooth, perfectly debris cleaned racetrack.* And unlike a racetrack, vehicles are moving in head-on directions when on a public two-way road! Keep that in mind when you're out there. Here are some of the possible hazards on any curvy public roadway:

Oncoming traffic

Debris on surface

Uneven pavement and potholes

Motor vehicles entering roadway

Narrow single lanes

Blind corners

Water and Ice

Wet metal surfaces

Crossing animals and pedestrians

Children at play

And much more

Curvy Roads:

Driving on curvy challenging roads certainly is one of the most popular and enjoyable driving experiences for motorcycle drivers. And with the popularity of lightweight high-speed racing-type bikes, those curves are especially fun.

And driving a motorcycle safely and confidently on any curvy roadway will require all of us to master the BASIC science of cornering.

To drive a motorcycle safely, it is **essential** that all drivers understand the basic science of tire traction, motorcycle balance, counter steering, and last, but certainly not least, proper cornering.

For the *Twisties* you need to be knowledgeable and ***dead confident* on HOW** to approach a corner, properly select a sound pathway, and choose a speed not only appropriate, but one you can handle.

There are many great books, talented teachers, and driving courses to learn from, but make no mistake,

'Cornering' is a basic fundamental task we all

need to master.

The following terms are examples of concepts

we all should be familiar with:

'Apex, Center of gravity, centrifugal force, decreasing-radius, increasing radius, lean angle, counterbalancing, countersteering, counterweighting, deceleration, lean angle, loads, low-side, high-side, and much more.'

(MSF Motorcycling Excellence by Motorcycle Safety Foundation, Whitehorse Press, 2nd ed., 2005, pg. 191/192)

From whatever sound source you are learning

from, such as this manual, you should assertively apply

what you learn to execute these methodologies properly

by practicing again and again. In time, you should

instinctively perform the appropriate action and master

the skill-set.

Your life will likely depend on it!

Chapter 6: Master the Use of Your Machine and Gear

Introduction:

Like me, anyone who has served in a military organization or even the Boy Scouts, understands that being **well trained and prepared** is extremely important to mission success, or even an overnight camping trip.

If you truly want to improve your odds out on the road, you need to not only get familiar with, but also drill yourself again and again using your machine, its essential devices, the optional accessories, and all your protective gear, such as apparel, gloves, and helmet.

Doing so will minimize the time to perform those tasks and maximize your time to fully focus on your driving.

Strategy:

I sometimes enjoy feeling like a military aviator fighter pilot, being intensely focused on my mission success of arriving alive with no crashes, and applying my skill-set, knowledge, and experience well, in the hostile environment of our roadways. Drilling myself on the usage of my equipment, and knowing its limitations, and mine, is essential for mission success—and returning home alive.

Proficiency and Maturity:

If you think getting your Motorcycle License makes you "road ready"... you are kidding yourself! Proper training and practice are what enhances your skill-set and proficiency. Always be evaluating your abilities and challenge yourself by improving.

Good mature judgment that concerns your well-being should allow you to bow out at times and choose not to make that bad decision. And again, when you experience an incident, you need to reflect and determine what is best to do next time in the same situation. And if you can't figure it out... read!

Examples:

This reminds me of two hair-raising experiences when I first started driving. Both had the factors of excessive speed. One was choosing to execute a dangerous high-speed pass. The second was taking on a turn too fast for my skill-set, while driving on some curvy mountain roadway.

The Pass

I recall the time I eagerly chose to pass a slower

moving Big Rig Truck. I misjudged the space and nearly had a head-on with a car! It was a stupid move on my part. I have practiced that move and now do it very confidently.

Cornering and excessive speed:

I recall the first time I really felt the hair on the back of my neck rise up. I took a corner way to fast and again nearly hit a car head-on. I executed the maneuver totally wrong, too fast, taking it way to wide and nearly causing me to cross over the centerline. Really shook me up!

I will never forget those incidents. They were the first significant 'close-calls' that I almost had serious consequences with. Cracking a book, watching videos, taking any driving course, and practicing new found methods is how anyone learns to master a skill.

The Machine:

A good start is to read the owner's manual. Get familiar with everything about it.

Proper maintenance is essential for your machine to perform at its optimal best. And operating your motorcycle properly is obviously beneficial. First, practice using everything you read about while you're still in the garage.

Get familiar with the location and use of electronic gadgets: horn, turn signals, radio, GPS, windscreen, cruise control, heated grips, and so forth. You want to memorize their locations and learn how to use them all.

Then go to parking lots and practice. I cannot emphasize enough how essential it is to bond and get familiar with your machine. Practice and drill yourself. Simple maneuvers can and should be done precisely and swiftly.

Shifting and Braking:

Look, listen, and feel the machine move through the gears. You need to be very familiar with your machine's ability and limitations, if any.

This is especially important when you're passing a vehicle, since you will have only a few seconds to perform the maneuver. You need to be very familiar with how the bike accelerates. Practice both passing safely and braking.

Become familiar with your motorcycle's braking equipment. Read up on the options of applying your front and back brakes.

And practice how to execute a complete, safe, high-speed emergency full stop in a safe place, such as in a formal motorcycle driving class and/or parking lot.

Some new bikes are equipped with ABS brake systems that work very well in preventing skidding. (Something to consider before you shop for bikes.)

Regardless of what type of brakes you have, you need to know how to fully stop on your machine. If you don't, you can be thrown from the bike! You can read all about this in many sources.

You also need to be prepared to stop your machine at *all* speeds and in *all* road and traffic conditions. That is why tailgating is such a bad idea. Creating and managing the proper space and time in front of you is essential to stopping safely.

I learned how to execute high-speed stops by enrolling in a standard motorcycle-driving course. And, as soon as I was eligible, I also enrolled in an advanced course. I strongly suggest you do the same ASAP.

Tip: Rob's Rule of Thumb for Shifting

When you're on a curvy road, and approaching a corner, remain in gear that matches the first digit of the posted YELLOW SIGN recommending the speed for each corner. Be in that gear *before you begin turning.*

Rule:

20/25= second gear

30/35=third gear

40=fourth gear

(Get familiar with your machine and your feeling of comfort with this. You can modify and create your own rule-of -thumb)

When done *smoothly*, the transmission downshifting and engine compression affect can securely control your bike and will certainly reduce brake wear. Again ... *smoothly* is essential!

Tires:

Get the best you can afford. And proper air pressure and tire condition are very important. Have proper flat-tire repair needs and proper lighting on hand. Getting a flat tire can happen in the dark and during the worst sort of weather.

Be prepared. I suggest you practice using the repair equipment and fixing a flat at home. Get a used tire from a cycle shop.

Also, have a towing plan with possible options

on where you might have the bike towed to for tire or mechanical problems. You will need to know that address. Perhaps you were given a directory of authorized service providers when you bought your bike? If not, I suggest you be prepared.

Apparel:

Basically, there are three types of conditions to be concerned with.

1—Dry, Cold Weather

2—Dry, Hot Weather

3—Wet, Rainy Weather

Here is the first thing to remember concerning apparel, you might have heard that most drivers who hit motorcyclists claim *they never saw us. So like many, when it comes to safety, choosing any bright*

colored clothing is a smart choice. And a bright colored

or white helmet will certainly help also! We all see

more drivers wearing bright-colors now for the obvious

safety benefits. Worth considering before you invest a

lot of money in gear.

For optimal comfort, safety and practicality,

consider wearing layers or a well-designed systems

jacket, with removable linings, and multiple vents and

pockets.

Many will have the opinion that leather apparel

is the toughest safest sort of apparel to wear. The

Racing Pros wear it, and Black Leather has been a

traditional apparel item for a long time. In fact, my first

jacket was a black leather one. Soon after, I dropped out

the black leather jacket for a bright color synthetic

material system & layer approach. Yet, I still do wear

padded leather racing pants.

1) For cold-climate driving, you might consider getting the outer shell jacket one size bigger to allow for additional layering. Also consider one of those electric, heated, plug-in liners/vests—that's my personal choice.

2) For hot weather riding you might consider a mesh-style jacket as another type of apparel item to select for optional wear. And if you do, consider wearing additional body armor underneath due to the less protective quality the mesh jacket material might provide.

I'm bringing all this up because being *comfortable, cool, warm, dry, and safe* will allow you to better focus on your driving.

Do you really want to be distracted because

you're cold, sweating, or soaking wet while driving around all day? I have been there done that.

From morning to noon, afternoon to evening, temperatures can vary a great deal. Consider where you will be riding. If you were planning on doing a lot of touring, the systems apparel would be your best bet.

3) Rain gear; there are lots of options here. My systems jacket has a Gortex waterproof lining and the outer shell is only *water resistant.* So that outer jacket gets soaked in a downpour. If you want to stay warmer and dry, you could consider buying a one-size bigger waterproof rain jacket to put over your existing as I do. Before I slip on the rain jacket, I open all vents on my other and, make certain my wallet is in an easy to access location. The opening of the vents will minimize and perhaps eliminate sweating from the humidity.

You might also consider a one to two size bigger waterproof pant liner too. Make sure the pants have large Velcro flaps to allow you to slip them on OVER your boots.

I put my waterproof rain gear out on the saddle so to speak, so I can pull over and access without delay or hassle.

Familiarity of Apparel:

Also, you need to be familiar with your apparel.

How do you unsnap a button or zip open, close, or vent the jacket?

And again, consider opening the back vents *before* you put it on! You will have to pull over and take off to do this obviously. Pays to think ahead!

Here's a good one: worried about that wallet or cell phone falling out of a pocket? In which direction do the zippers move to close a pocket on your jacket? How about your helmet air vents? Doing any of these tasks while driving has a *factor of risk.*

I suggest you consider doing only the absolute essential things while driving. The more practiced you are in doing these simple tasks, the safer you will be.

Apparel Tips Review

Jacket: a brightly colored, heavy-duty, well-vented, pocketed, and padded leather or synthetic jacket

Pants: padded and vented are ideal. Leather, synthetic, or color? You decide.

Electric vest/jacket liner: I'm never cold with my thermostat-controlled device. It makes driving extremely comfortable and allows me to focus better.

Gloves: don't skimp here. Forget fashion and logo-embossed gloves. Buy for fit, comfort, quality, and function.

Eyewear: get the best you can afford, what you need and like...and wear them.

Waterproof layer: stow away inexpensive waterproof shell and pants (get oversized—one to two sizes bigger—to slip *over* what you're wearing). Most motorcycle pants have enlarged ankle Velcro bottoms that allow you to easily slip them on right over your boots.

Ear protection: I never ride without it! You can still hear—it just cuts the nonessential road noise out and allows you to concentrate.

Wearing them will save your ears!

Practicality, function, comfort, and safety are more important than fashion.

Chapter Conclusion

Again, it is important that you practice using everything you think is essential while actually driving. So practice safely while stationary at first, then while driving in a parking lot, and finally, when you're on the road.

And certainly don't practice when you have a passenger. In fact, don't take a passenger until you're way beyond the beginning stage of driving a motorcycle.

You want to remain focused on your primary task, driving. Practice and arrive alive without incident.

Chapter 7: Be Alert, Engaged, and Scan for Potential Hazards

Be alert, engaged, and scan for any potential hazards. Developing and perfecting this essential habitual behavior, is primary to achieve the desired results of a safe journey without any incidents. Any risk-ratio reduction strategy cannot evolve without this behavior focus.

Never consume alcohol while driving.

When you're tired, rest, or call it a day.

Always scan the roadway in all four zones to be prepared for any unexpected hazard.

And again, scan as far as you can, using both your eyes and ears. Just because you can't see or hear it, doesn't mean the danger doesn't exist.

Know now, that to expect the unexpected, you must be engaged at all times and allow your knowledge, experience, and imagination instinctively work together. Relax, focus, and enjoy the ride!

Strategy:

To be alert and engaged, we need to focus on our primary goal. #1 Goal: AAWI / Arrive Alive Without Incident!

We need to remind ourselves of this each time we get on our machines, ***one ride at a time.*** Driving from location A to destination B.

Think about the things you ***can*** control out there on the road—

Your attitude and behavior.

Your driving focus of reducing risk.

Your speed.

Your management of the zones around you.

Your management of your lanes, other vehicles, and your options.

Your knowledge, skill level, experience, and confidence.

What you know and how you apply that knowledge

Being prepared.

And...**anticipating and, expecting the unexpected!**

Chapter 8: Continue to Learn and Practice

The benefit of continuing to learn and practice should be obvious, and should make sense to you. Just subscribing to any good cycle publication and reading product reviews, travels, etc., etc., will bring a higher level of thought. Besides, zoom in on articles of motorcycle riding and safety.

I choose to take a California DMV (Dept. of Motor Vehicles) Motorcycle course before I got my 'M' class license.

And I am happy to share I even took the advance course twice!

The fact is, I don't think of myself as a hotshot

driver. But, I do think of myself as a very concerned and conscientious one! And to further hone your driving skills, also consider the experience of real Track-Time! The experience of driving on a track will be amazing and educational with any motor vehicle.

Conversations regarding accident experiences with other motorcycle riders will always be enlightening.

The huge benefit with a continuing education focus is-- you don't have to truly experience everything firsthand to learn. *That means you don't need to get in a motorcycle accident to learn about them.* Again, listen to the stories, evaluate the information, and be careful who you take advice from. Not all drivers are safe drivers.

Attitude on Self-Teaching:

Little by little, you can push the envelope with new knowledge and focused practice. This will improve your skill and confidence a great deal. But, right after you experience a 'hair-raising' incident; get in the habit of analyzing what just happened.

If it's especially hair-raising, then, if it's possible and safe, I suggest you actually pull over and think about the close call. A perfect time to take a break and really think about what happened.

Ask yourself...

"What just happened there? "

"What could I have done to better anticipate that? "

And better yet...

"How could I have better anticipated that to have avoided the incident altogether?"

Other Examples...

Could you have been driving more slowly?

Did you anticipate the driver's behavior poorly?

Did you see all of the other driver's options?

Blame Game:

Don't get in the habit of believing your own bullshit when it comes to motorcycle riding.

The fact is much of what happens in the Universe is out of our control.

And we can count on all human beings making lots of mistakes.

The bottom line is the 'blame-game' is for fools

and the dead! So don't become a ***foolish dead guy!***

Learn and create safe habits early on, and break the bad ones. You don't want to build a foundation of false confidence from bad, even crazy, habits.

Chapter 9: Conclusion:

So much can be said about the joys of motorcycle driving. And like most, I truly love to ride regardless of the dangers.

A friend of mine recently asked, "Why do you choose to ride knowing how dangerous it is?" The simple answer I gave him was I love the feeling, excitement, and enjoyment it brings me.

Now here is the much better answer to the same question: "Why do you choose to ride knowing how dangerous it is?"

I drive because of the extraordinary enjoyment I get, due to the challenges and unique human perspective I experience, while driving only a motorcycle can provide.

The complex feelings, regardless of the known dangers, are exhilarating and rewarding to me personally. And at times, the emotional experiences are even spiritual to me.

Examples of those pleasurable moments are when I'm driving through or near a challenging or perhaps beautifully breath-taking roadway environment.

Such as:

Driving on a smooth paved, dry, curvy road up and down a mountain pass, or driving along a river basin, or driving along a cliff-hanging roadway!

Or driving during a sunrise, or sunset. Or driving along an ocean coastline. Or driving in a vast desert.

Another example would be enjoying the natural cool temperature of a cool forest on a very hot day.

And finally, the exhilarating experience of driving a huge Majestic Mountain walled valley!

Those are the really special experiences that I seek and crave more of.

I also love the fun, excitement, challenge, camaraderie, and, of course....*the speed!* Those are the reasons why I choose to drive a motorcycle!

In closing, I wish to end where I started.

I wish to stress the point that no matter how many decades of experience we drive, no matter how many hundreds of thousands of miles we put under our belt in the saddle, and no matter how well we master the task of driving our machines, any

motorcycle driver, and/or passenger, can get

seriously injured or die while riding!

Good luck, God's speed, and while focusing on the ride,

from point A to point B, strive to—**Arrive Alive**

without Incident! RJ

The 9 Essential Concepts Revisited

[Figure 7: The 9 Medallion]

1-Risk-Ratio-Reduction Strategy

2-Four Zones

3-Space & Time are relative

4-Anticipate & Expect the Unexpected

5-Lane Management

6 Sharing the Road

7-Be instinctively aware

8- Focus on your well-being

9-Self Critical Analysis & Self Teaching

(Expanded clarification of these 9 concepts are found on pages: 16-18)

AAWI: Arrive Alive Without Incident

RRRS: Risk Ratio Reduction Strategy

www.arrivealivewithoutincident.com